Alphabet

TRACE THE LETTERS

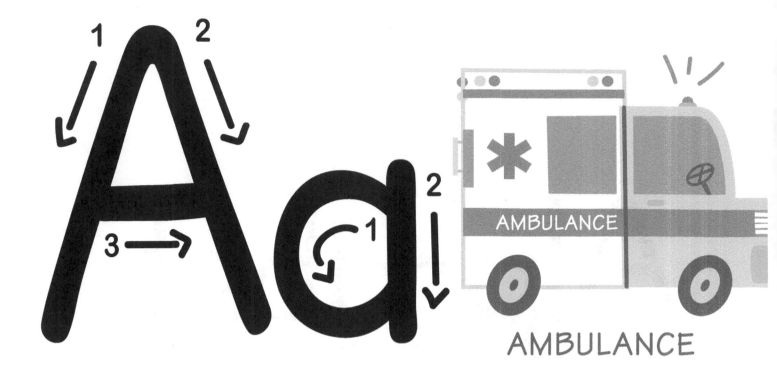

AMBULANCE

ambulance

a a a a a a a a

A A A A A A A A

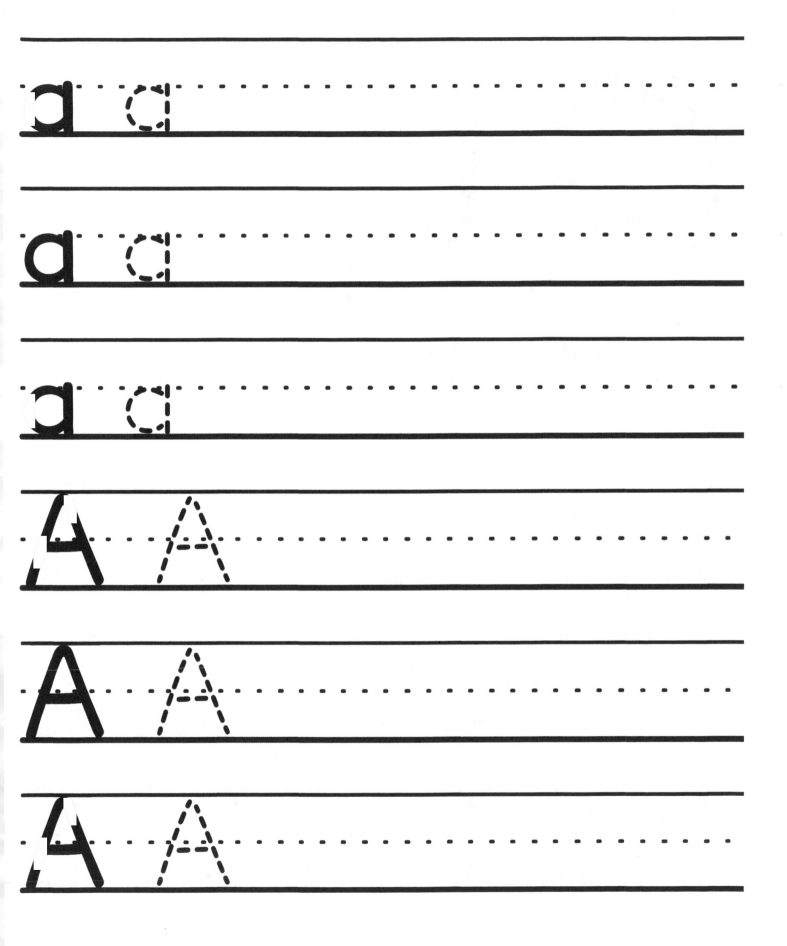

BIPLANE

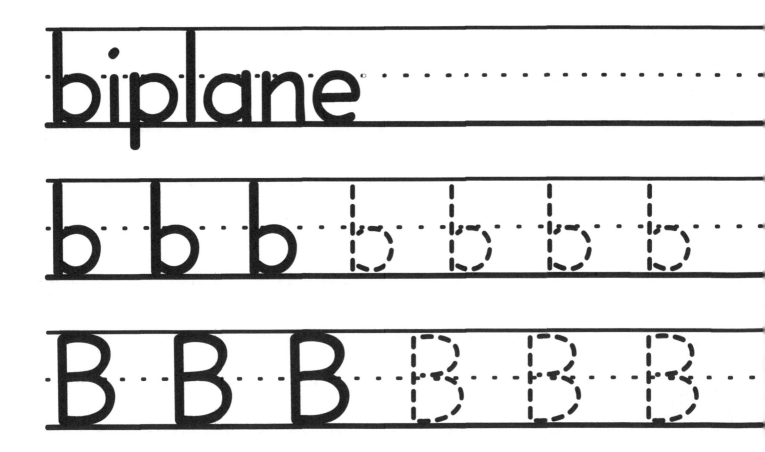

biplane

b b b b b b b

B B B B B B B

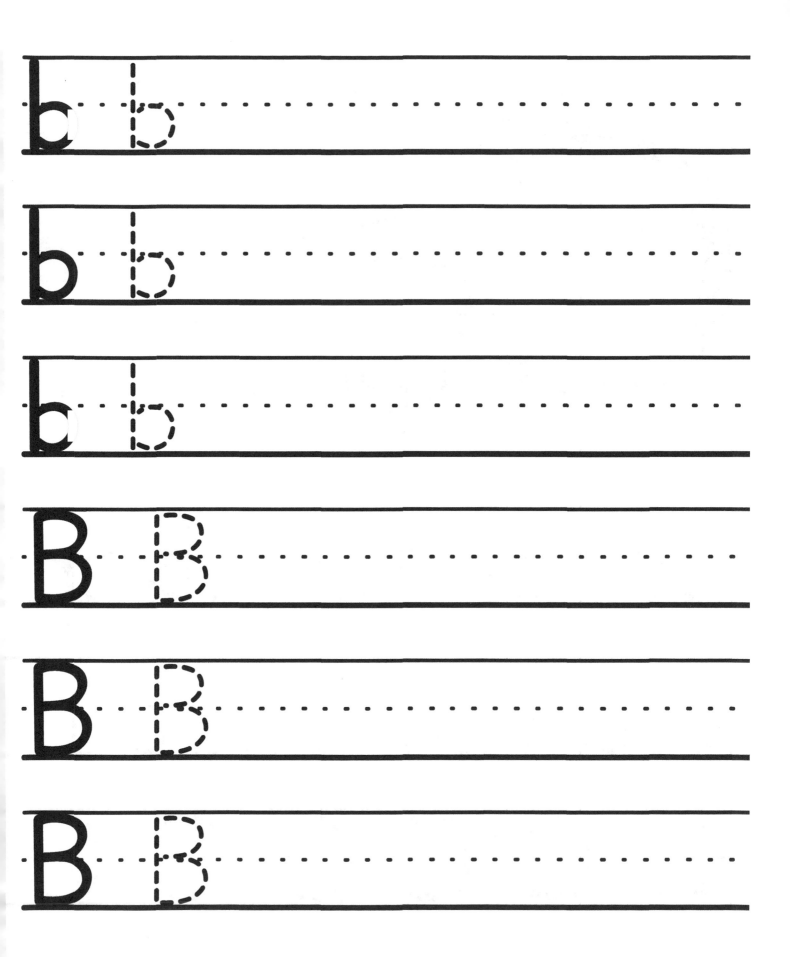

CONCRETE MIXER TRUCK

concrete mixer

c c c c c c c c c c

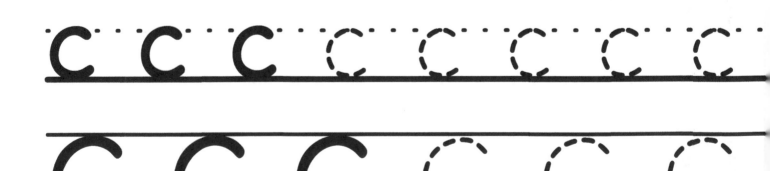

C C C C C C C C

DUMP

dump truck

d d d d d d d

D D D D D D D

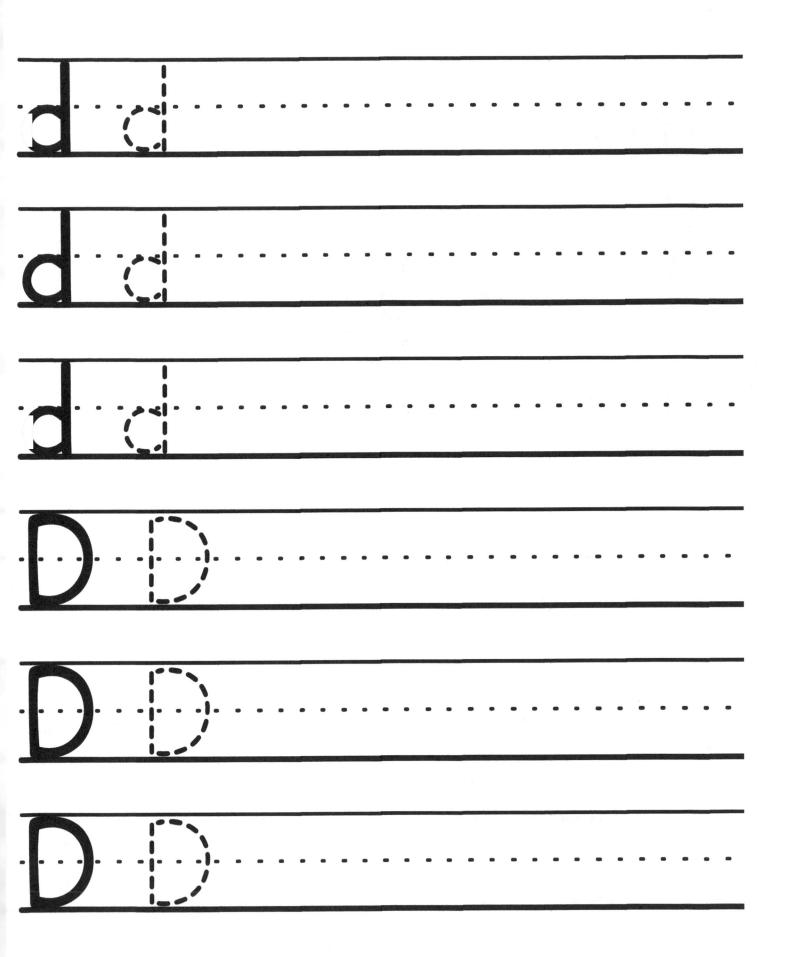

EXCAVATOR

excavator

e e e e e e e e e

E E E E E E E E

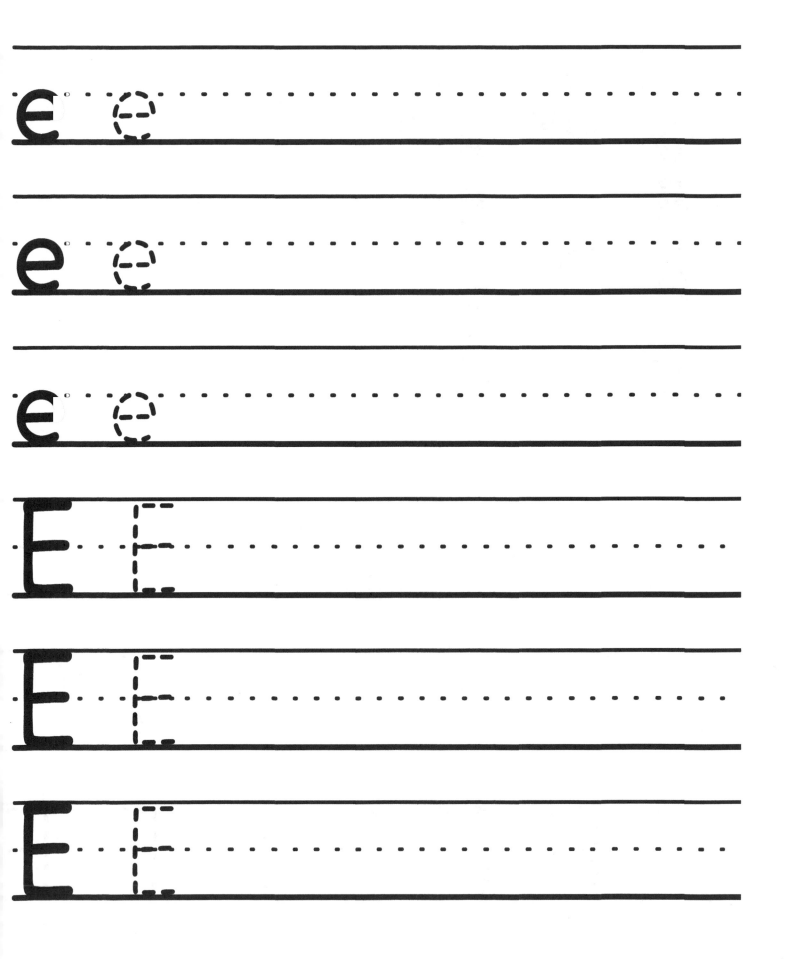

FIRE-ENGINE

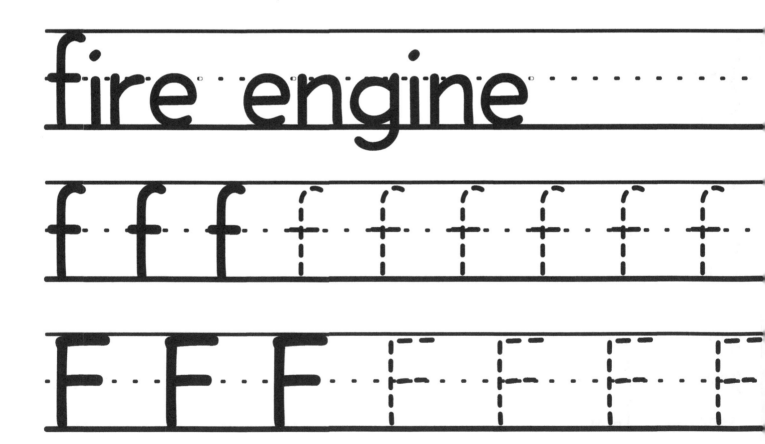

fire engine

f f _____

f f _____

f f _____

F F _____

F F _____

F F _____

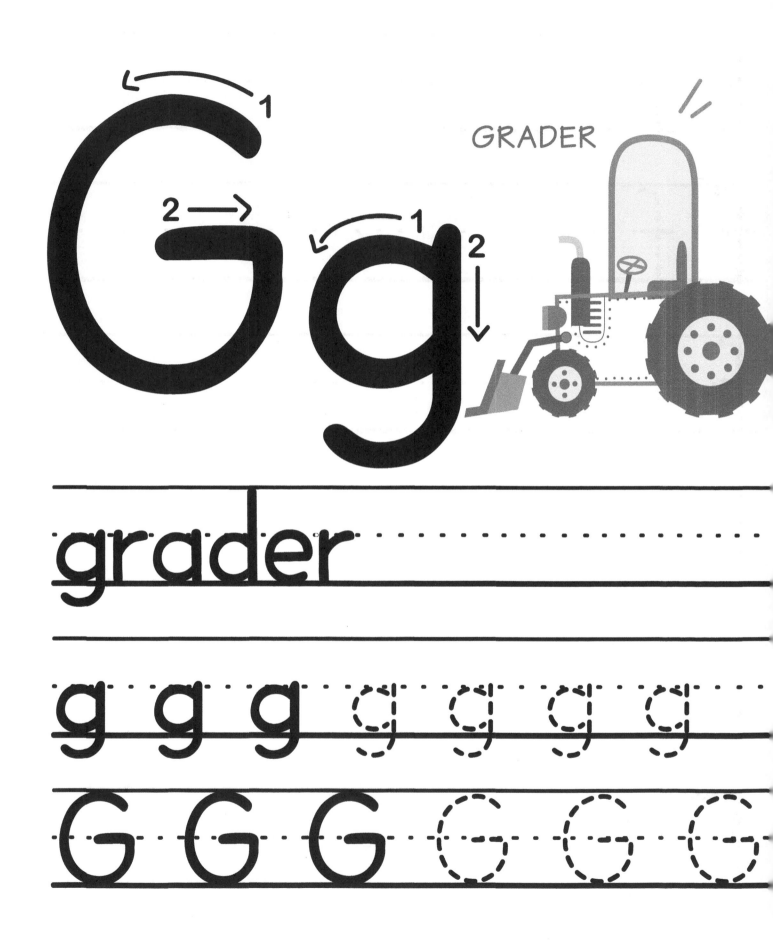

GRADER

grader

g g g g g g g

G G G G G G G

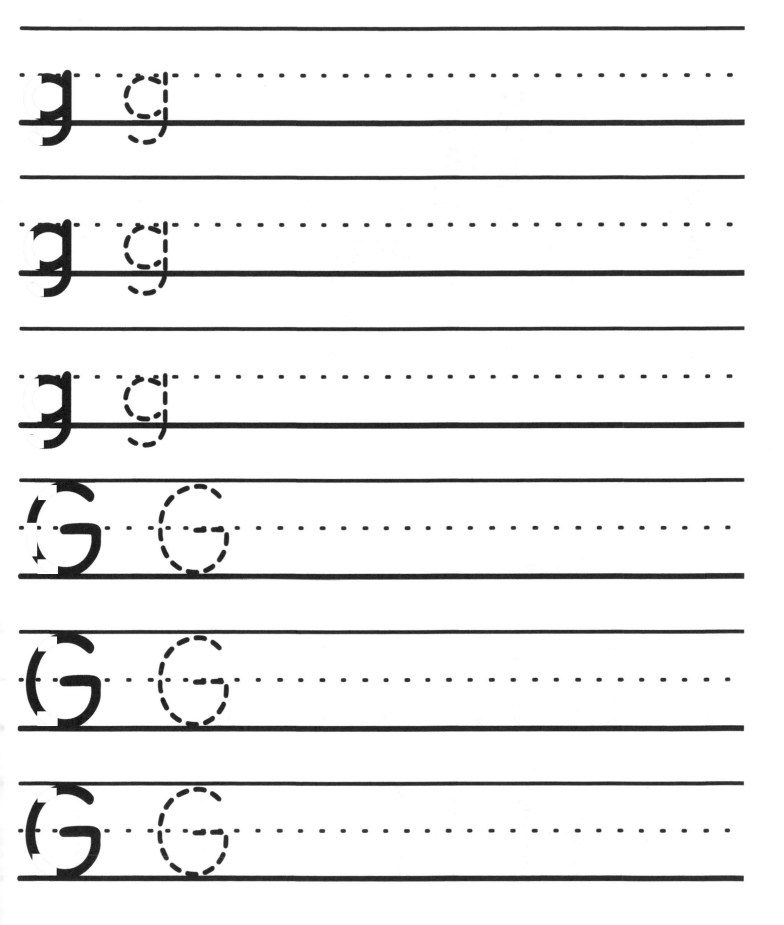

HELICOPTER

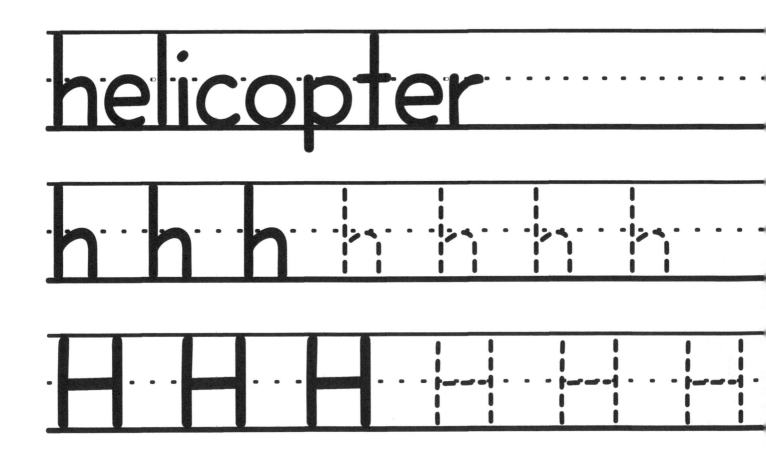

helicopter

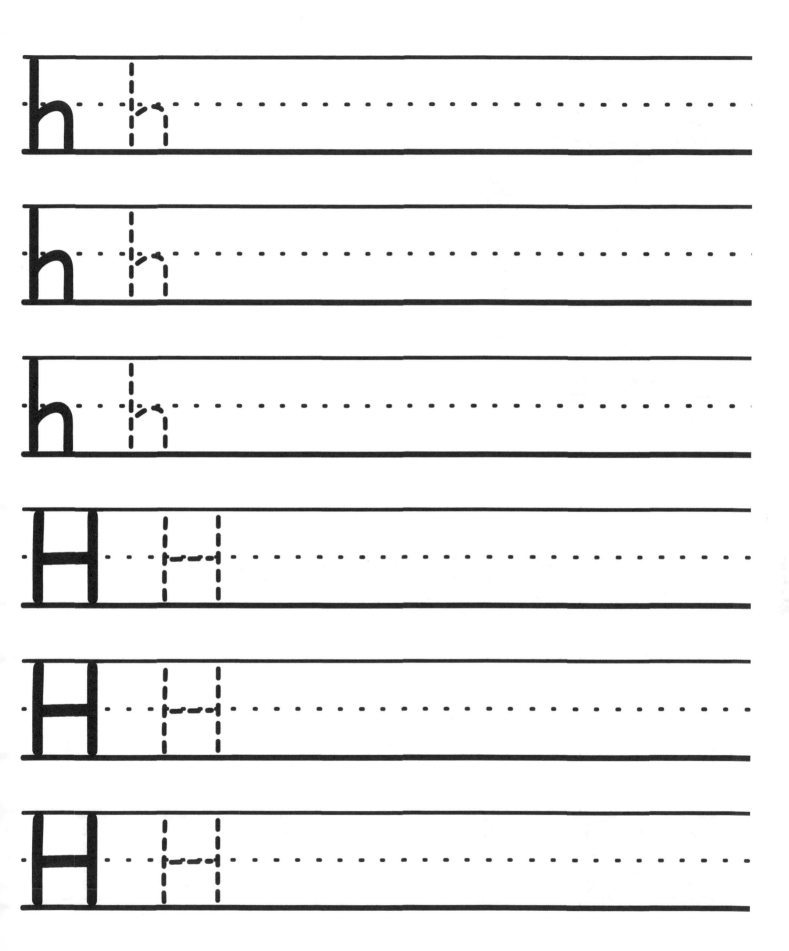

ICE
BREAKER

ice breaker

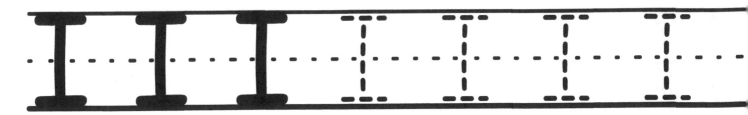

i i

i i

i i

I I

I I

I I

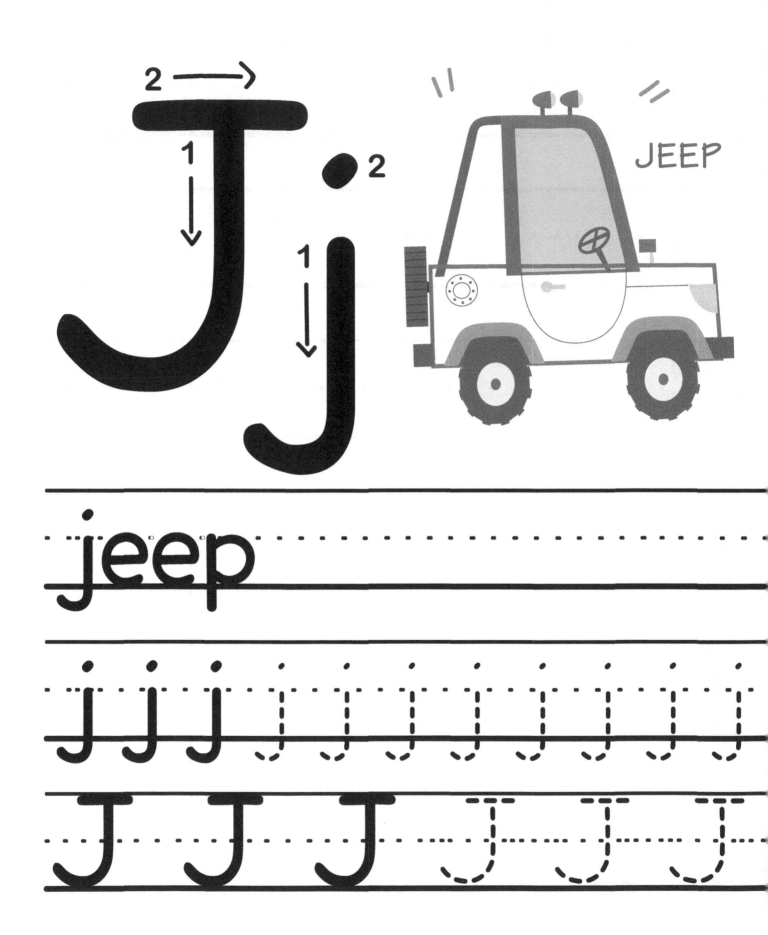

JEEP

jeep

j j j j j j j j j j j

J J J J J J J

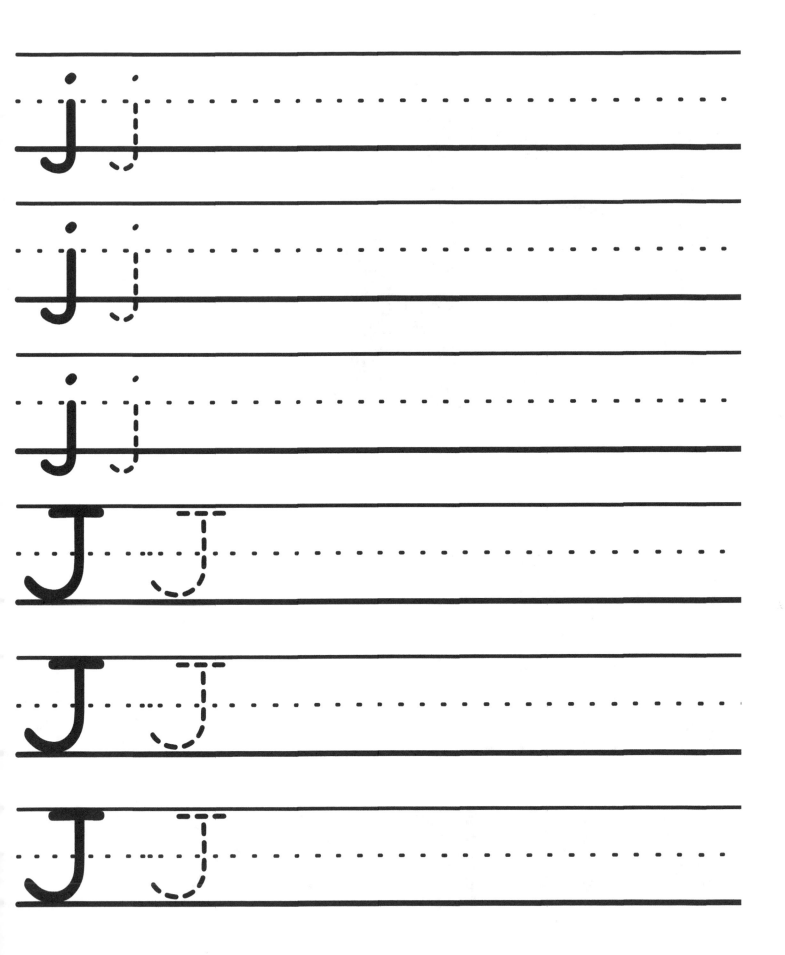

KAYAK

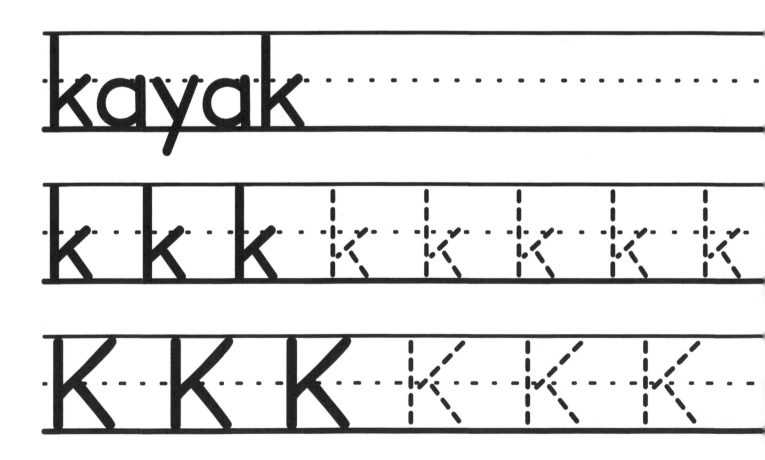

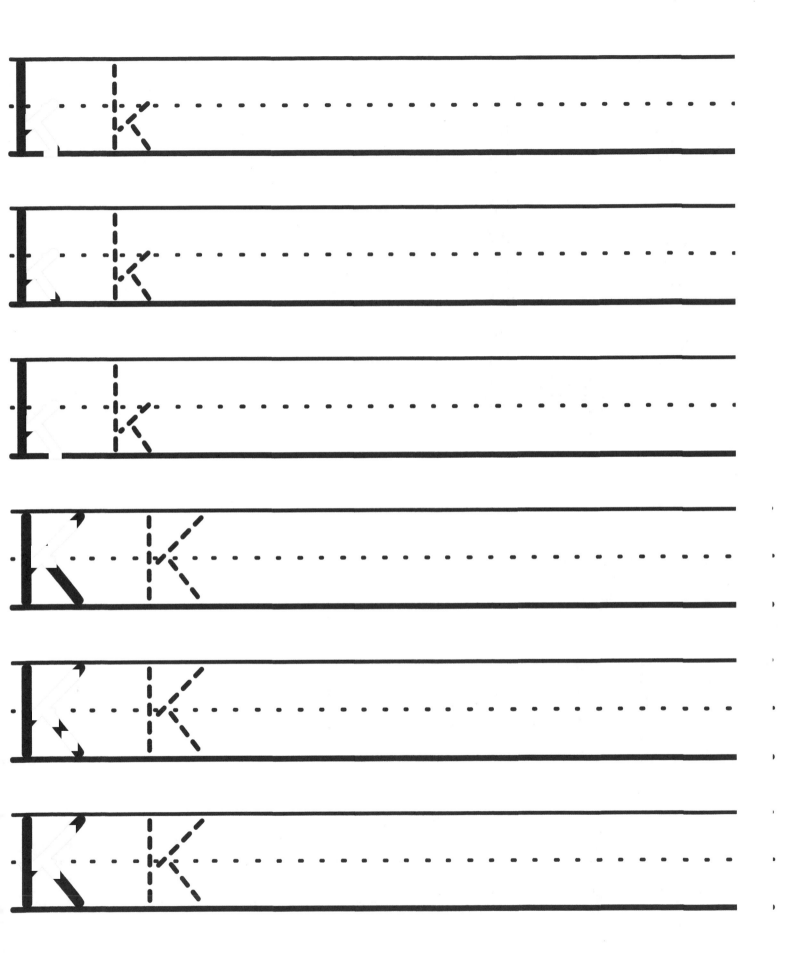

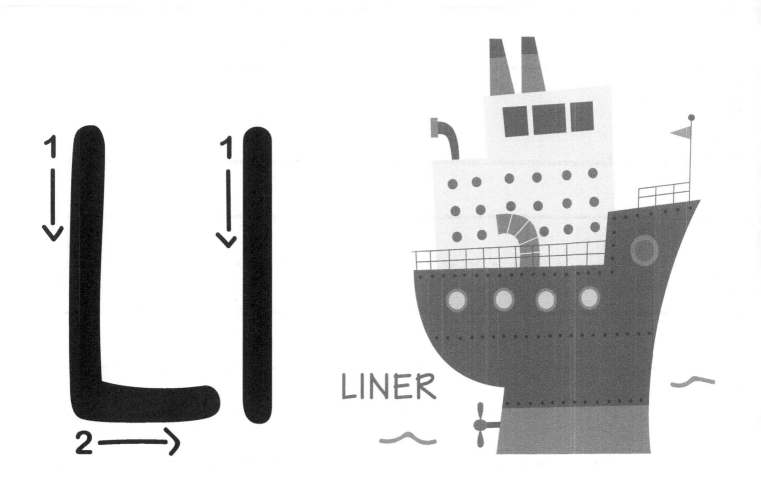

LINER

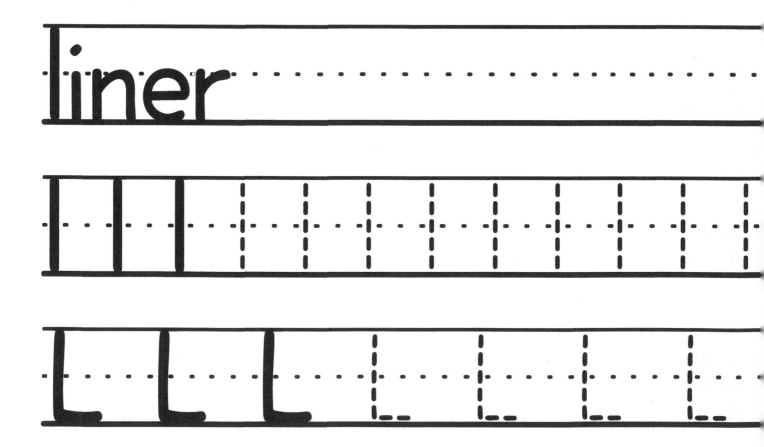

liner

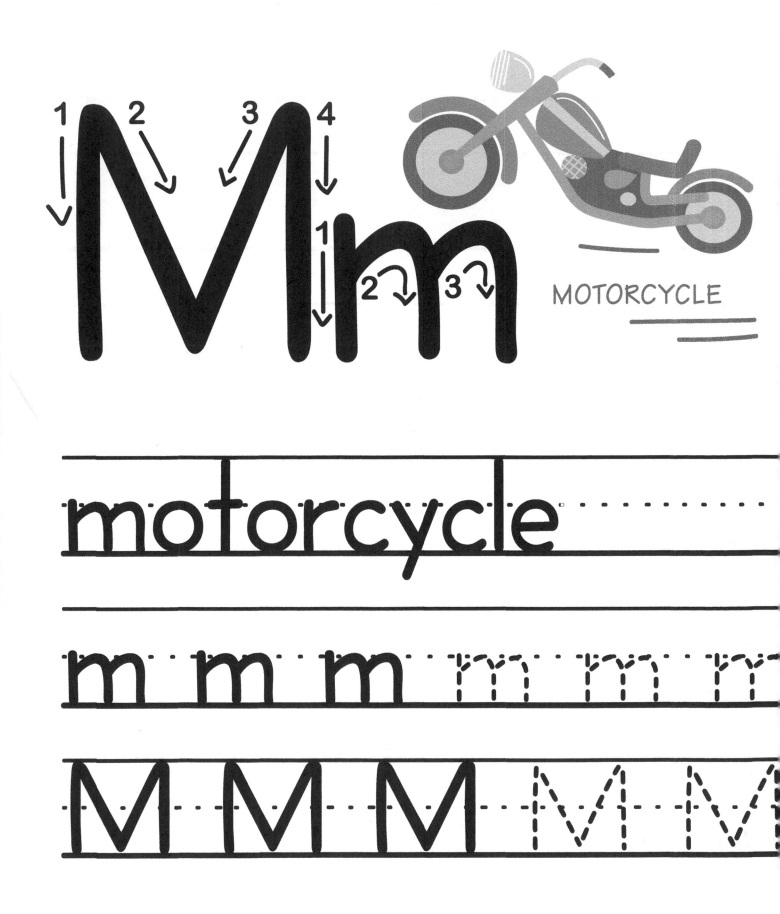

MOTORCYCLE

motorcycle

m m m m m m

M M M M M M

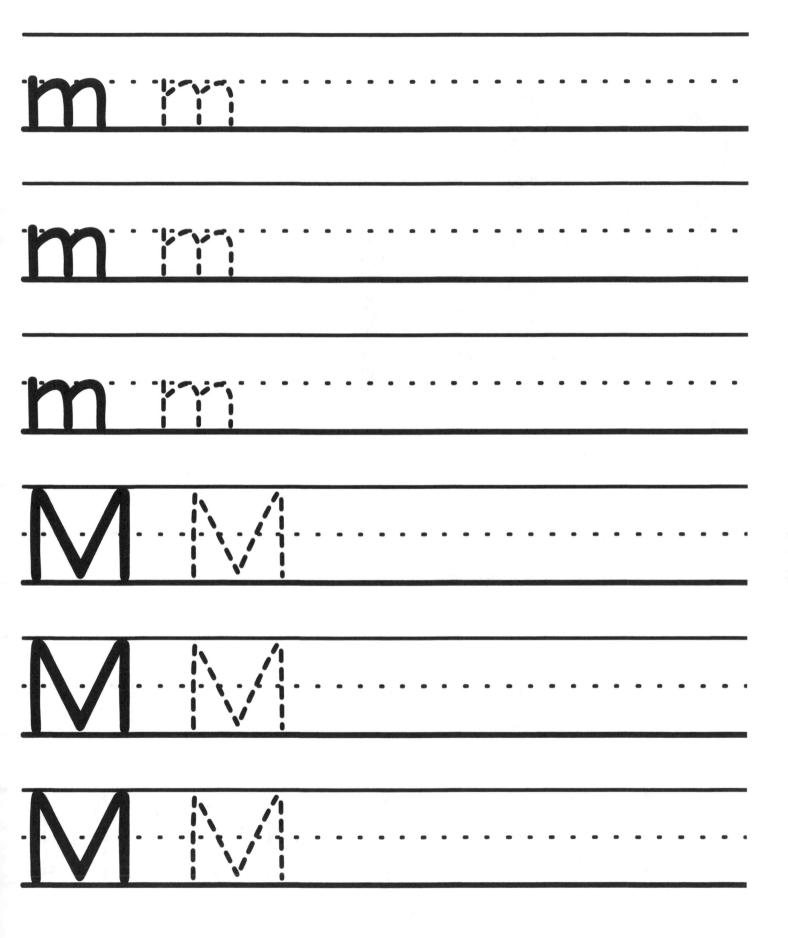

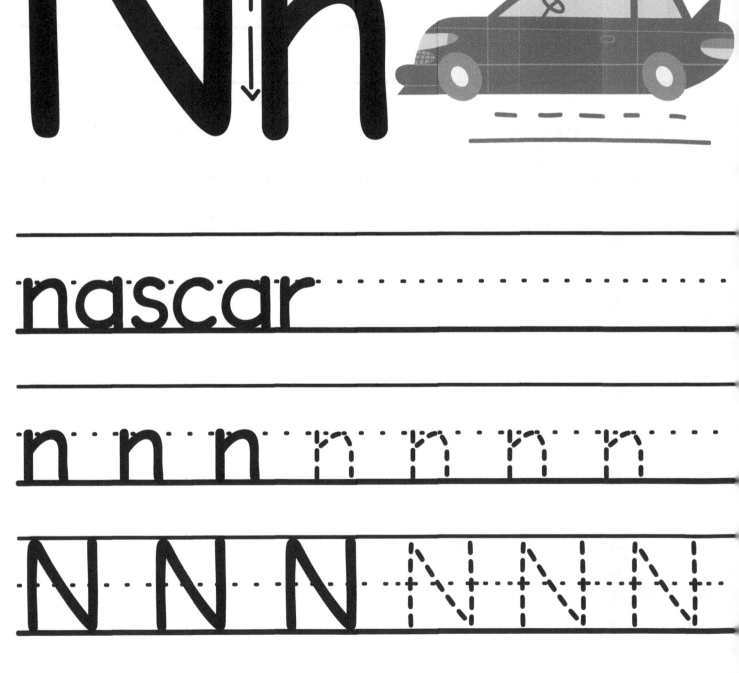

NASCAR

nascar

n

N

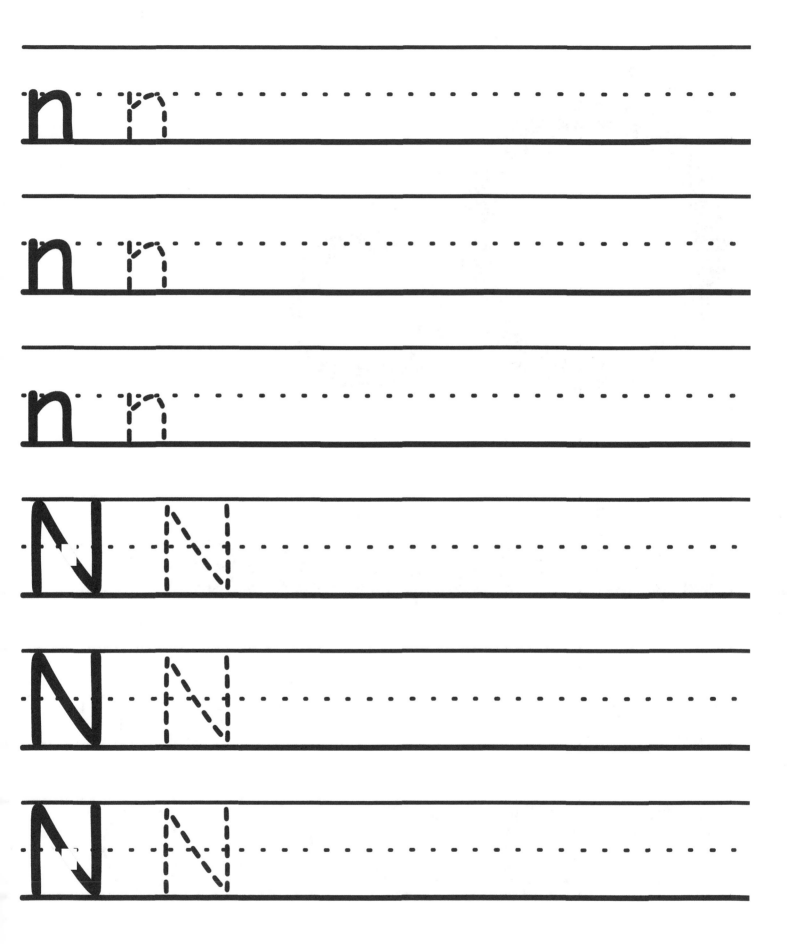

O

1

o

1

OLD
AIRPLANE

old airplane

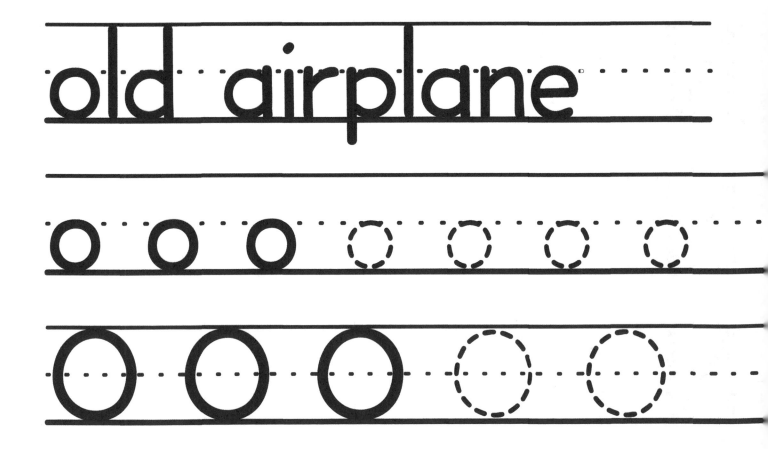

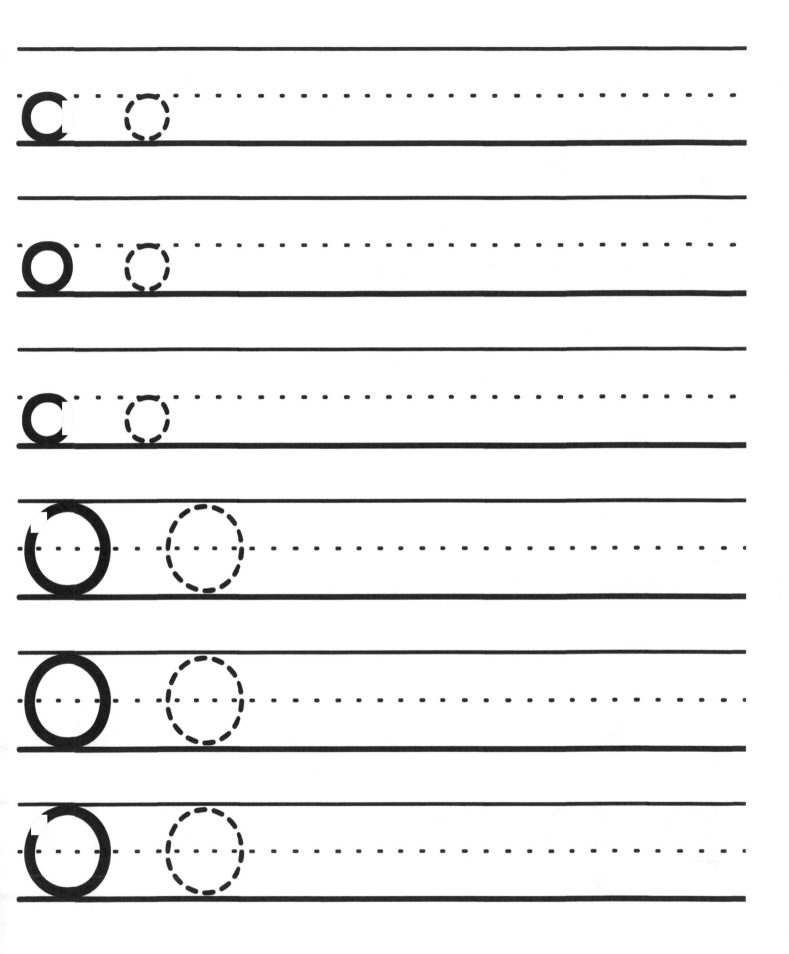

POLICE CAR

POLICE

police car

p p p p p p p p

P P P P P P P P

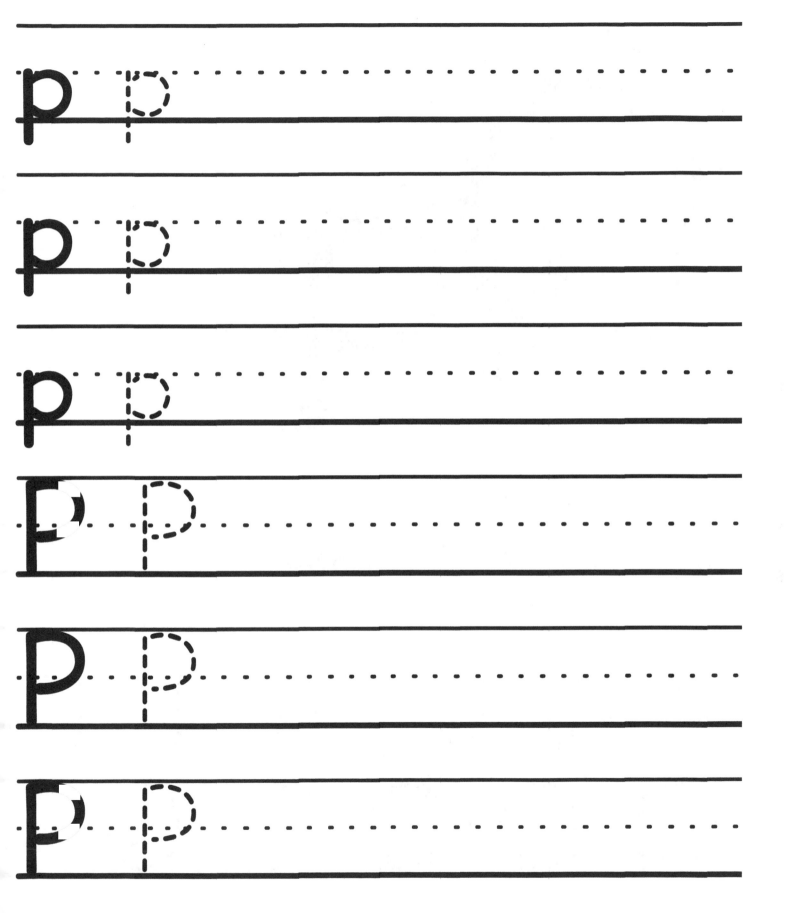

QUAD BIKE

quad bike

q q q q q q q

Q Q Q Q Q

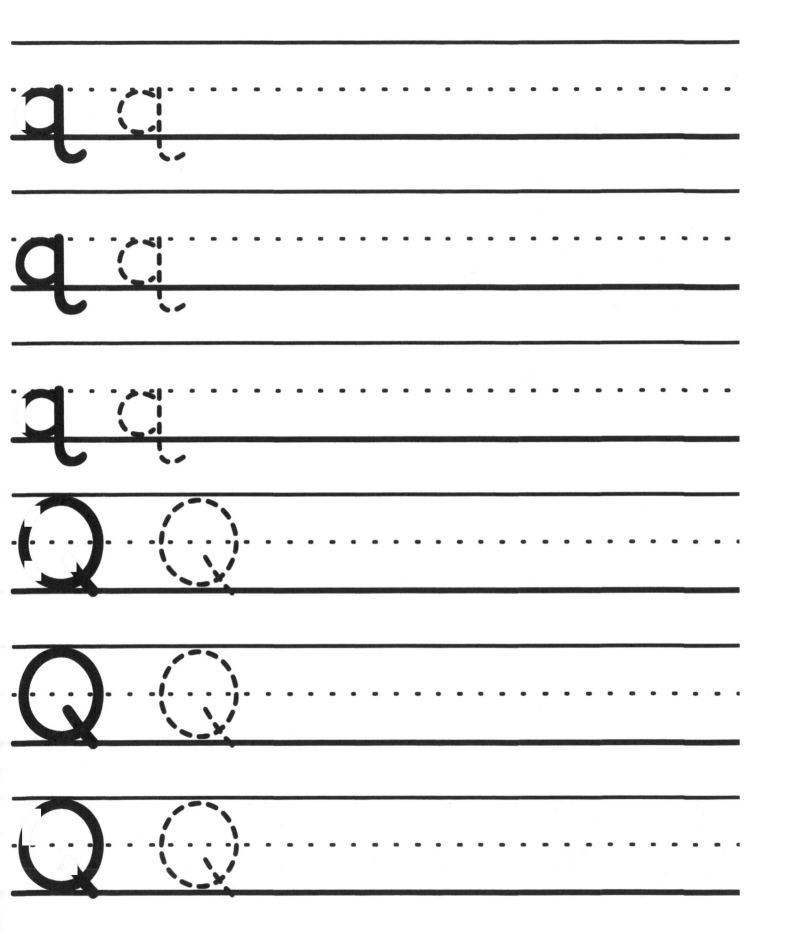

RETRO CAR

retro car

r r r r r r r r r

R R R R R R R

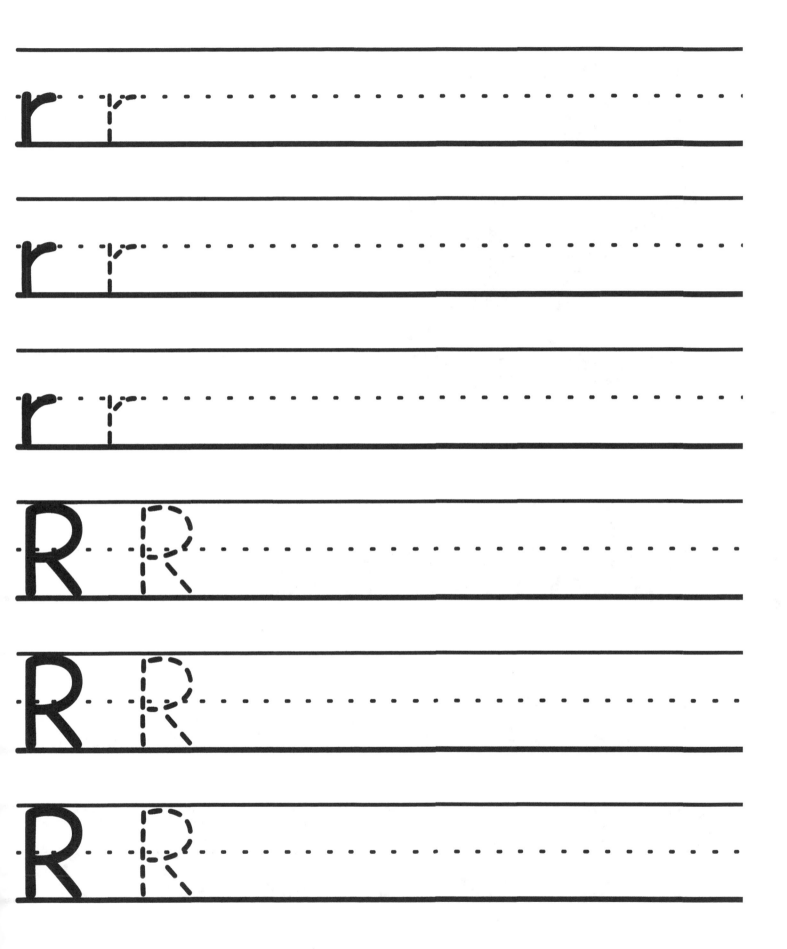

SUBMARINE

submarine

s s s s s s s s s

S S S S S S S S

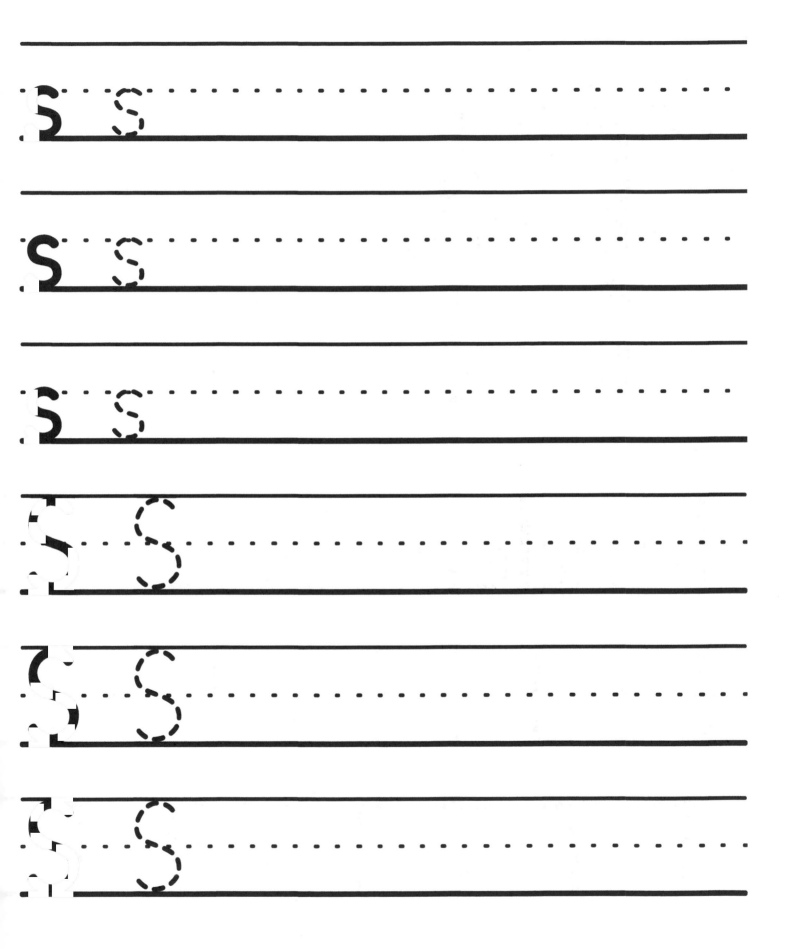

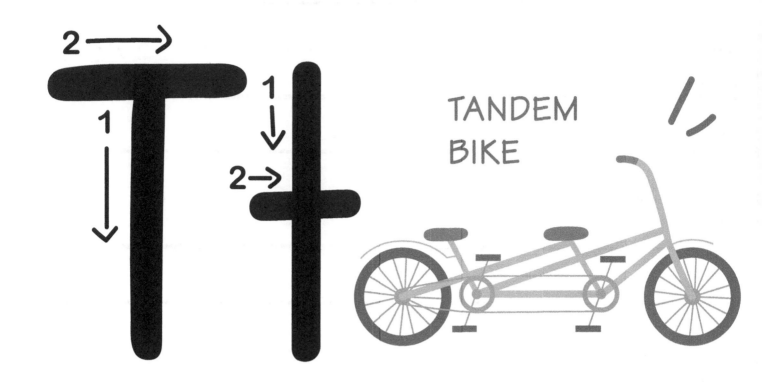

T t

TANDEM BIKE

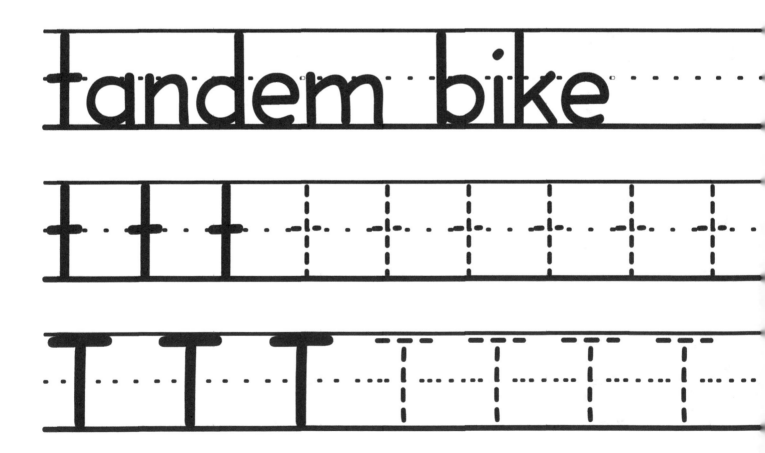

tandem bike

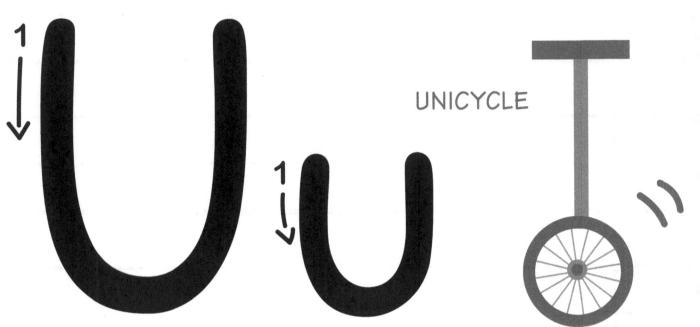

UNICYCLE

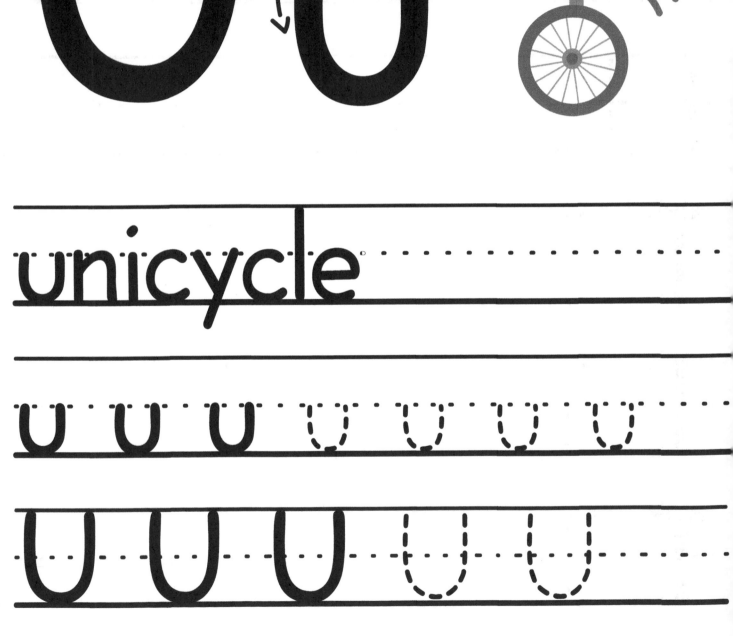

unicycle

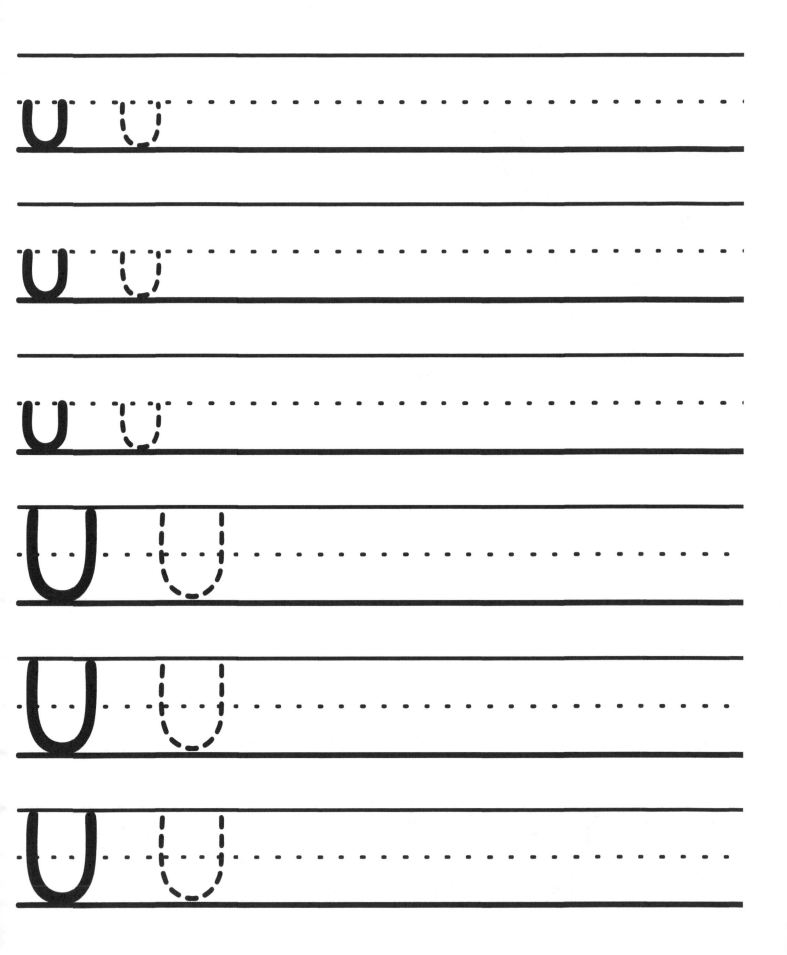

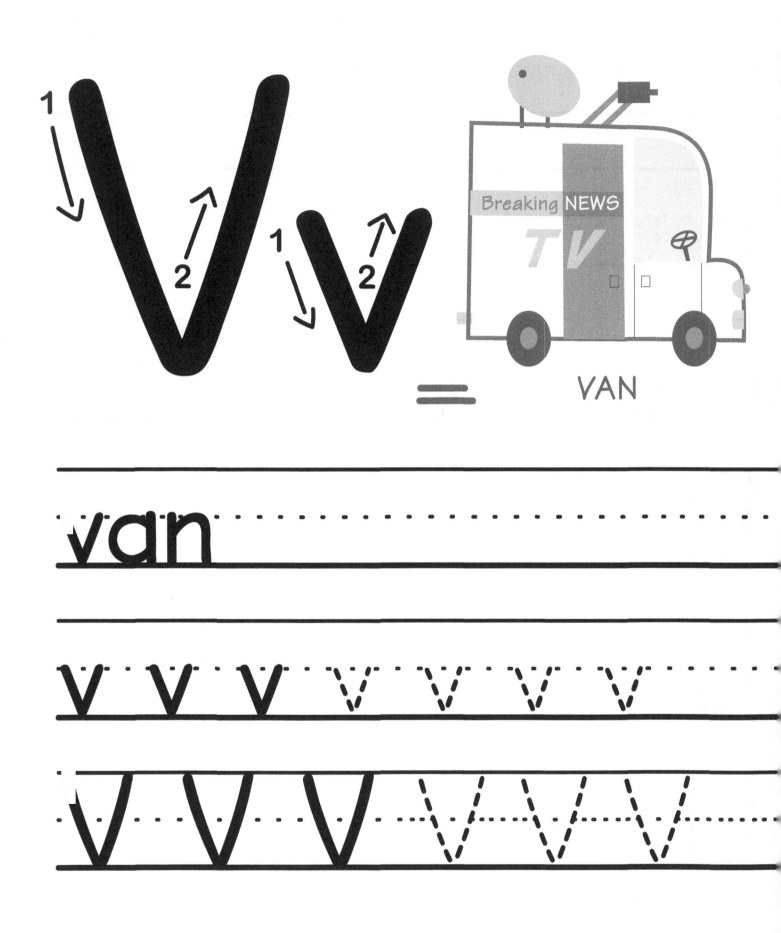

Breaking NEWS

TV

VAN

van

v v v v v v v v v

V V V W W W

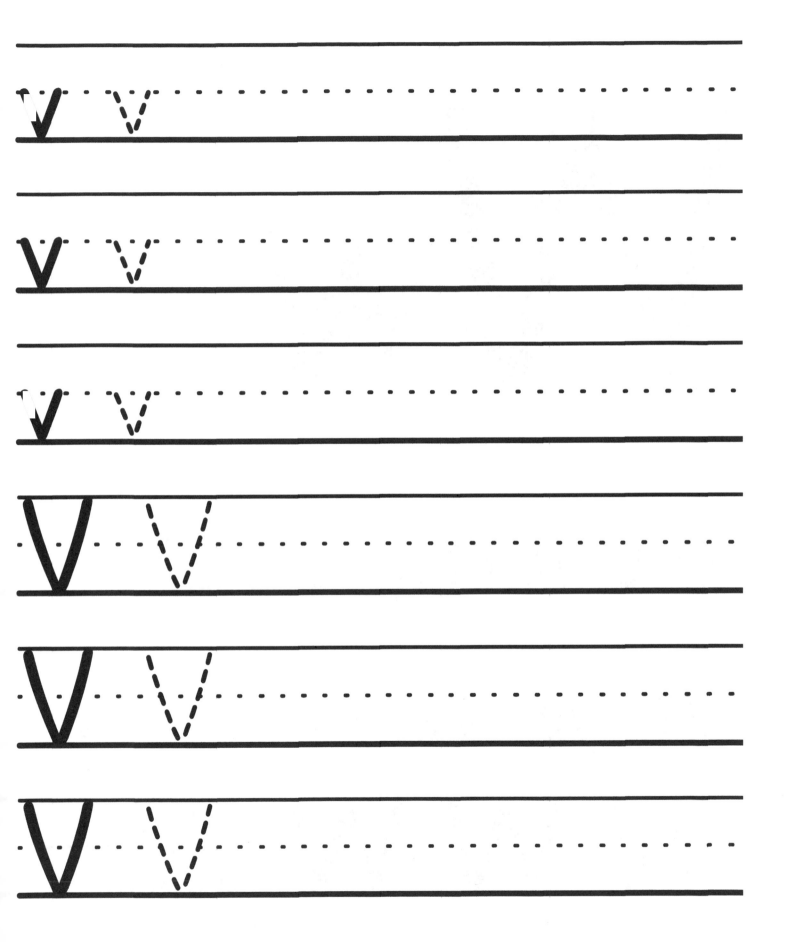

WALKING
BOAT

walking boat

w w w w w w w

W W W W W

W w W w

W w W w

W w W w

W w W w

W w W w

W w W w

X-MAS SLEIGH

x-mas sleigh

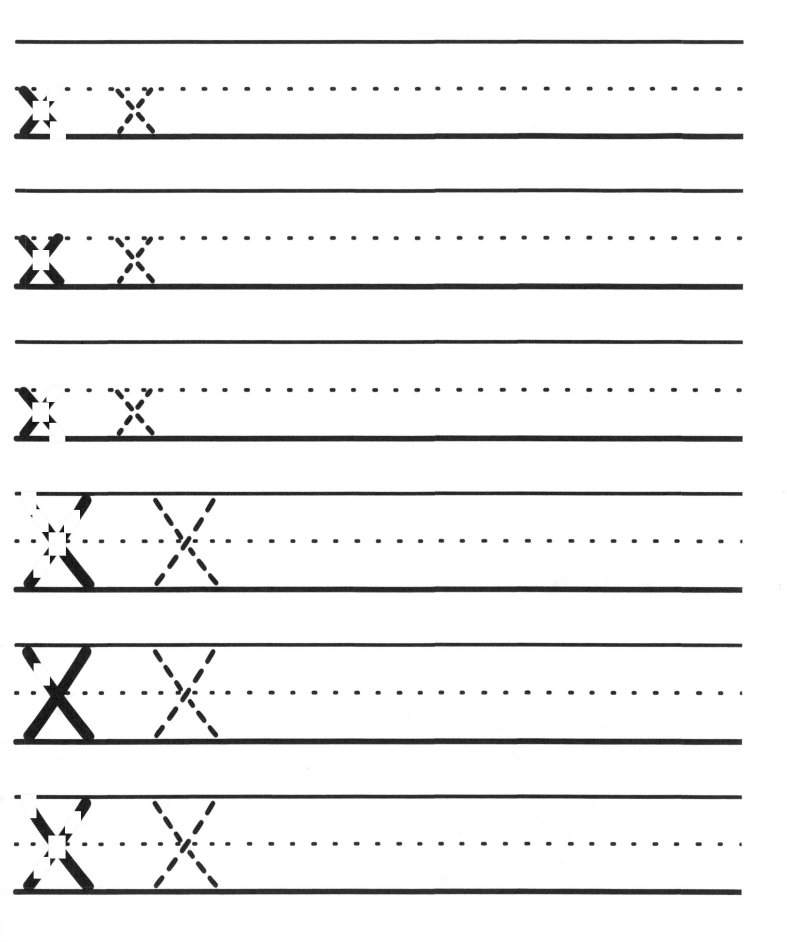

YELLOW TAXI

TAXI

yellow taxi

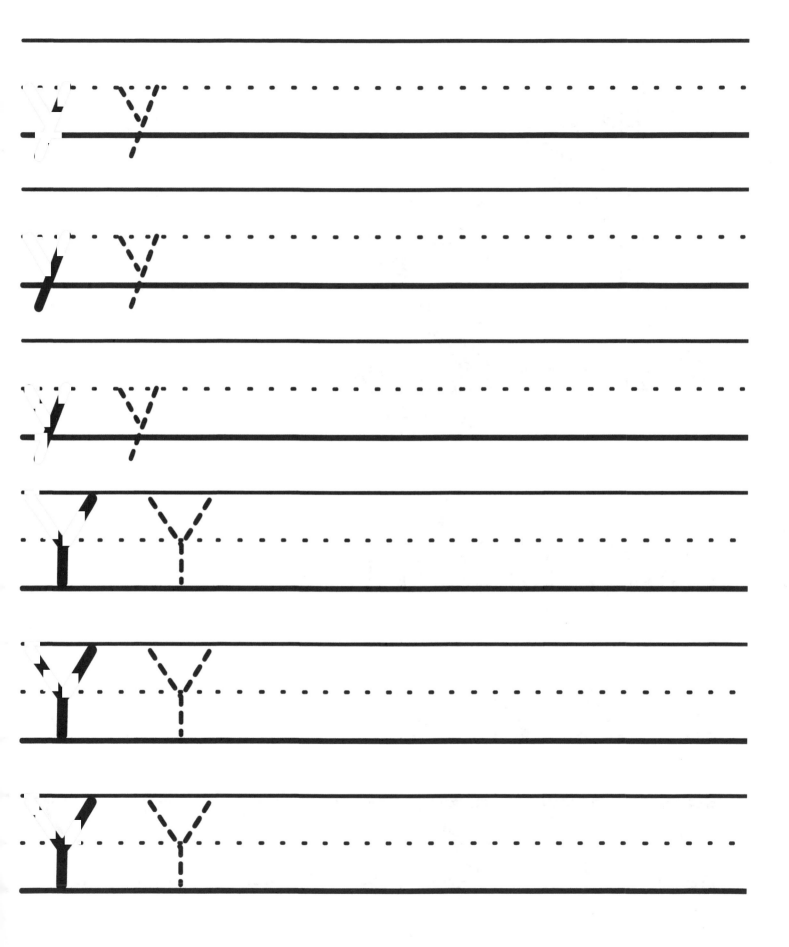

ZEPPELIN

zeppelin

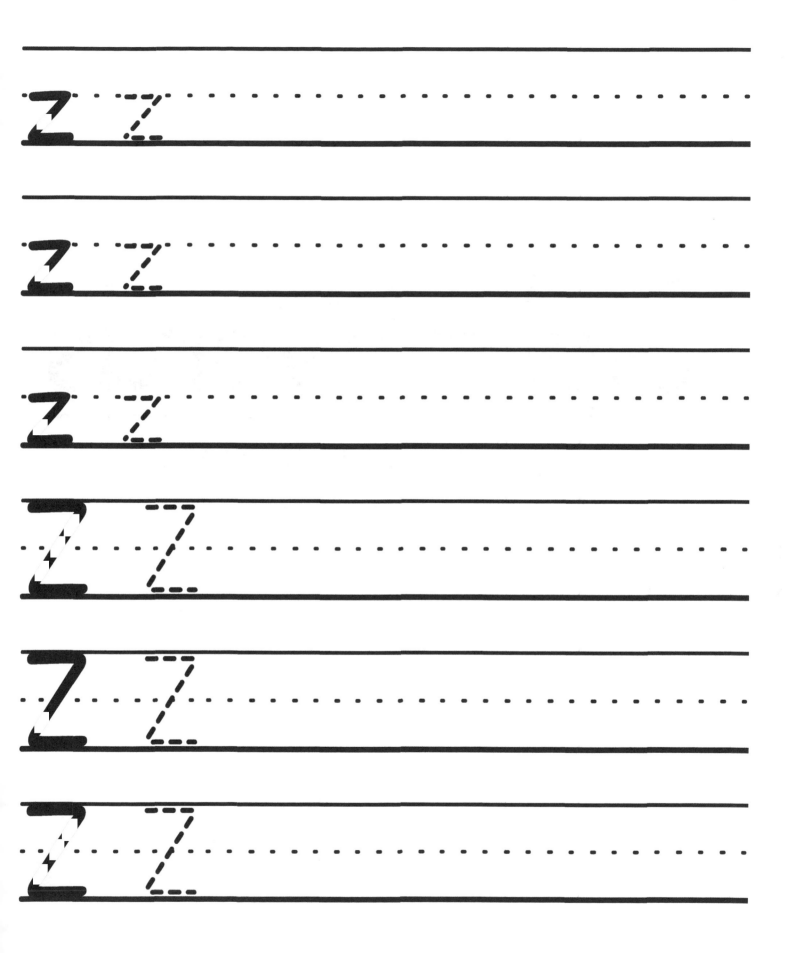

Sight Words

LEARN TO READ

Aa is for...

Trace the word and say it aloud:

a a a a a a a

Write the word:

Trace the word and say it aloud:

am am am am

Write the word:

Trace the word and say it aloud:

and and and

Write the word:

Bb is for...

Trace the word and say it aloud:

big big big big

Write the word:

Trace the word and say it aloud:

blue blue blue

Write the word:

Trace the word and say it aloud:

be be be be be

Write the word:

Cc is for...

Trace the word and say it aloud:

can can can

Write the word:

Trace the word and say it aloud:

come come

Write the word:

Trace the word and say it aloud:

came came

Write the word:

Dd is for...

Trace the word and say it aloud:

do do do do do

Write the word:

Trace the word and say it aloud:

did did did did

Write the word:

Trace the word and say it aloud:

down down

Write the word:

Ee is for...

Trace the word and say it aloud:

eat eat eat eat

Write the word:

Trace the word and say it aloud:

every every

Write the word:

Trace the word and say it aloud:

eight eight

Write the word:

Ff is for...

Trace the word and say it aloud:

for for for for

Write the word:

Trace the word and say it aloud:

from from from

Write the word:

Trace the word and say it aloud:

find find find

Write the word:

Gg is for...

Trace the word and say it aloud:

go   go   go   go   go

Write the word:

Trace the word and say it aloud:

get   get   get   get

Write the word:

Trace the word and say it aloud:

good   good   good

Write the word:

Hh is for...

Trace the word and say it aloud:

help help help

Write the word:

Trace the word and say it aloud:

here here here

Write the word:

Trace the word and say it aloud:

have have have

Write the word:

Ii is for...

Trace the word and say it aloud:

I   I   I   I   I   I   I

Write the word:

Trace the word and say it aloud:

it   it   it   it   it   it   it   it

Write the word:

Trace the word and say it aloud:

is   is   is   is   is   is   is   is

Write the word:

Jj & Kk are for...

Trace the word and say it aloud:

jump jump jump

Write the word:

Trace the word and say it aloud:

just just just

Write the word:

Trace the word and say it aloud:

know know

Write the word:

Ll is for...

Trace the word and say it aloud:

look look look

Write the word:

Trace the word and say it aloud:

like like like like

Write the word:

Trace the word and say it aloud:

little little little

Write the word:

Mm is for...

Trace the word and say it aloud:

me me me me me

Write the word:

Trace the word and say it aloud:

my my my my my

Write the word:

Trace the word and say it aloud:

make make make

Write the word:

Nn is for...

Trace the word and say it aloud:

no   no   no   no   no

Write the word:

Trace the word and say it aloud:

not   not   not   not

Write the word:

Trace the word and say it aloud:

new   new   new

Write the word:

Oo is for ...

Trace the word and say it aloud:

on on on on on

Write the word:

Trace the word and say it aloud:

one one one

Write the word:

Trace the word and say it aloud:

our our our our

Write the word:

Pp is for...

Trace the word and say it aloud:

play play play

Write the word:

Trace the word and say it aloud:

put put put

Write the word:

Trace the word and say it aloud:

please please

Write the word:

Rr is for...

Trace the word and say it aloud:

red red red red

Write the word:

Trace the word and say it aloud:

run run run run

Write the word:

Trace the word and say it aloud:

ride ride ride

Write the word:

Ss is for...

Trace the word and say it aloud:

see   see see see

Write the word:

· · · · · · · · · · · · · · · · · ·

Trace the word and say it aloud:

said said said

Write the word:

· · · · · · · · · · · · · · · · · ·

Trace the word and say it aloud:

some some

Write the word:

· · · · · · · · · · · · · · · · · ·

Tt is for...

Trace the word and say it aloud:

to to to to to

Write the word:

Trace the word and say it aloud:

the the the the the

Write the word:

Trace the word and say it aloud:

that that that

Write the word:

Uu & Vv are for...

Trace the word and say it aloud:

up up up up up

Write the word:

Trace the word and say it aloud:

us us us us us

Write the word:

Trace the word and say it aloud:

very very very

Write the word:

Ww is for...

Trace the word and say it aloud:

was was was

Write the word:

Trace the word and say it aloud:

with with with

Write the word:

Trace the word and say it aloud:

we we we we

Write the word:

Yy is for...

Trace the word and say it aloud:

you you you you

Write the word:

Trace the word and say it aloud:

your your your

Write the word:

Trace the word and say it aloud:

yes yes yes yes

Write the word:

Practice!

Practice!

Practice!

Practice!

Practice!

Practice!

Practice!

Practice!

Practice!